Original title:
Clover Chronicle

Copyright © 2025 Creative Arts Management OÜ
All rights reserved.

Author: Alexander Thornton
ISBN HARDBACK: 978-1-80566-683-7
ISBN PAPERBACK: 978-1-80566-968-5

Serendipity Amidst the Blades

In a field where laughter grows,
Waddle of ducks and sneaky toes.
Bumblebees dance, oh so spry,
While grasshoppers chirp a cheeky hi.

A rabbit slips, oops, there it goes,
Chasing shadows, wearing woes.
Amidst the blades, joy springs forth,
In this green carpet of mirth and mirth.

Fables of Fields and Fortune

Once a snail with dreams so bright,
Hid its shell, thinking it light.
Every turn, a tale unfolds,
With twists of laughter, never old.

A wise old owl set the scene,
Telling stories, witty and keen.
Fields of mishaps, silly and grand,
Every fortune, a funny hand.

The Enchanted Clover Trail

There's a path where giggles flow,
With pixies dancing to and fro.
A frog in a hat sings off-key,
Making flowers chuckle with glee.

Stumbling gnomes in a silly race,
Falling down, but still in grace.
Under rainbows, laughter prevails,
On this whimsical, clovered trail.

Echoes of Nature's Bounty

Breezy whispers in the air,
Squirrels argue without a care.
The bumblebees hum a tune,
While raccoons dance 'neath the moon.

Jokes from the owls float on by,
As fireflies blink in reply.
Echoes of laughter, bright and free,
Nature's joy, a comedy spree.

The Alchemy of Green Whispers

In the garden, whispers play,
Laughter sprouting every day.
Mischief hides beneath each bloom,
Tickling toes in nature's room.

Bees are buzzing, jokes take flight,
Dancing shadows, pure delight.
Petals giggle, colors shine,
Sunlight winks, a cheeky sign.

Leaves play tag with clouds so fast,
Rooted stories from the past.
Beneath the green, tales unfold,
Silly secrets, bright and bold.

With every step on grassy turf,
You'll find a laugh, a joyful surf.
Nature's jesters, bright and spry,
Come join the fun, oh me, oh my!

Leafy Dreams and Stardust

In a land where leaves conspire,
Dreams take flight, a wild choir.
Bouncing thoughts from tree to tree,
Sprinkled stardust, oh what glee!

Twirling through the emerald maze,
During nights, the fairies blaze.
Silly laughter fills the air,
Joyful spirits, everywhere.

Wishes ride on breezy flows,
Tickled toes in nightly shows.
The moon's a jester, with a grin,
Urging dreams to let life in.

In the garden of delight,
Leafy dreams take wing in flight.
With every rustle, hear the sound,
Of laughter blooming all around!

Through the Lattice of Leaves

Through the leaves, a journey starts,
Witty whispers, playful hearts.
Glimpses of the world below,
Silly secrets, nature's show.

Each branch a tale, each stem a joke,
The wind may laugh, the branches poke.
In the shade, a merry band,
Of critters join, together stand.

Leaves like pages, turning fast,
Sharing stories, unsurpassed.
With every rustle, giggles rise,
Nature's party in disguise.

Through the lattice, joy takes flight,
Brighten up the starry night.
In the dance of green and gold,
Find the laughter in the bold!

The Volume of Verdant Lore

In a book made out of leaves,
Tales are spun, each word deceives.
Jokes and riddles, fresh and bright,
In the heart of nature's light.

Every word a silly twist,
In the garden, can't resist.
Pages flip as breezes blow,
Whispered secrets, gentle flow.

Tales of roots and flying seeds,
Wondrous stories, nature leads.
From the soil to fluffy clouds,
Laughter blooms within the crowds.

So join the tale, feel the cheer,
Nature's voices, loud and clear.
The volume high, the foolish fun,
Beneath the sky, for everyone!

The Lush Symphony of Now

In a field where greens collide,
The tunes of laughter softly glide.
A squirrel twirls, a bird does chat,
While daisies dance beside the fat.

A bouncy frog leaps to the beat,
With hops that make the ground feel sweet.
They sing of sunshine, joy on loan,
As playful whispers fill the phone.

The breeze plays tricks, it pulls a prank,
A hat misplaced upon a tank.
A picnic checkered, crumbs all round,
A feasting frenzy, what a sound!

So gather close, let joy resound,
In nature's arms, where mirth is found.
We'll play our parts, in this great jest,
With smiles light as clouds at rest.

Threads of Luck in the Wilderness

Among the twigs, a ribbon bright,
It tickles branches, takes to flight.
A raccoon pauses, a grin so wide,
With treasures hidden, he seeks to hide.

Oh fortune's favor, tangled be!
In every nook, a chance to see.
A ladybug with dreams so grand,
Plans journeys long across the land.

The compass spins, a dance of fate,
As chipmunks chatter, hardly wait.
They share the tales, of luck they've spun,
In nature's playground, just for fun.

So tie a knot, let luck be free,
In every thread, a mystery.
With laughter shared, and spirits warm,
In whispered woods, we weather the storm.

Sonnets of the Shamrock Vales

In valleys green, where giggles flow,
The sunbeams chase the shadows low.
  A butterfly with winks just right,
    Flutters past, on a whimsy flight.

Each shamrock whispers tales of glee,
  With snippets of what could just be.
    A jester's hat upon the dog,
  As frogs croak out in playful fog.

The valleys echo, "Come and play!"
Where silly bastions bravely sway.
  A rabbit's hop, a tumble fumble,
In nature's court, we laugh and stumble.

So raise a cheer for joy that grows,
  In every petal, laughter flows.
This merry dance beneath the trees,
  Is stitched in tales of joy and tease.

Tales of Flora and Fortune

Once upon a bloom, a tale unfolds,
Of daisies bold and stories told.
A sunflower grins, in golden cheer,
While bees conspire to buzz near.

The clover winks, a secret sly,
With four leaf whispers passing by.
In haphazard ways, they find their chance,
As petals sway in a silly dance.

A mouse with scissors, oh what a sight!
Trims the grass to dance at night.
With twirling shadows, laughter chimes,
And echoing jokes of simpler times.

So gather round, let stories sprout,
In every bloom, there's joy about.
These tales of flora, love and jest,
Bring fortune's hand, the very best.

In the Embrace of Green Dreams

In fields where greens collide,
The grass is my trusty guide.
I trip on fluffy four-leaf luck,
Watch out for that mischievous duck!

Dreams wander in fragrant bloom,
Bouncing high with every zoom.
The wind whispers jokes on repeat,
While ants march with tiny feet.

Sunbeams dance, all in a row,
As butterflies steal the show.
The earth chuckles, and so do I,
With laughter stitched in the sky.

The Elegy of the Enchanted Field

A weedy mess, or so they say,
But, oh, what fun in disarray!
Each tangle tells a tale so grand,
Of brave little bugs taking a stand.

The daisies wink, the bees all buzz,
Each moment filled with joyful fuzz.
Grassy whispers to me at night,
Be careful of the moon's delight!

An elf with mischief in his eye,
Declares war on a lonely pie.
In a realm where giggles soar,
I can't help but dream of more.

Serendipity's Fields of Green

Stumbling on a patch of cheer,
Where laughter bubbles, loud and clear.
Kites tangle in the sky so blue,
As ducks parade in mismatched shoes.

Beneath a tree, a gnome makes stew,
With odd ingredients, and a few.
What's that? A pie just flew by me!
A party with squirrels, can it be?

The laughter rolls like fluffy clouds,
Among my very silly crowds.
With every giggle, joy expands,
In this enchanted land of hands.

Secrets Under the Shamrock Skies

In the hush of twilight's embrace,
A jester's grin lights up the place.
Underneath a sky so wide,
The world's oddities cannot hide.

A rabbit hops with crazy flair,
While turtles dance without a care.
The stars above wink with delight,
As ants hold feasts in sheer twilight.

Dandelions giggle with the breeze,
Tickling thoughts like playful tease.
So secrets bloom where joy is sown,
In this field where smiles have grown.

The Poetry of Four Leaves

In the field where green things grow,
A squirrel with a grand to-do.
He dances round with quite a flair,
Chasing shadows in the air.

A grasshopper with a top hat bright,
Claims he's king from morning 'til night.
He sings a tune that makes folks giggle,
While the daisies sway and wiggle.

A snail in boots slides on a trail,
He's on a quest, but oh so slow.
With binoculars in his shell,
He thinks he's got it all in tow.

And when the sun begins to fade,
The critters join in a parade.
With laughter ringing through the trees,
They toast with dew to the evening breeze.

Fables of the Green Pastures

A cow in shades relaxes wide,
As sunbeams dance upon her side.
She moos a tune, like hip-hop beat,
And chews her cud while tapping feet.

A rabbit with a cap of red,
Claims he'd race but stops instead.
With carrot snacks and fans around,
He shares tall tales of leaps he found.

The chickens gossip, cluck and brag,
About a cat who lost her rag.
They've started rumors, much to cheer,
While strutting proud, devoid of fear.

The meadow hums with silly sounds,
As friendship grows from leaps and bounds.
With every hop and twirl of grass,
They laugh as all the moments pass.

Breath of the Leafy Realm

In the woods where whispers creep,
An owl jokes before his sleep.
With glasses on his beaked face tight,
He reads the stars like pages bright.

A mouse in pants tells tales so tall,
Of cheese so big, it doubled his wall.
His friends just chuckle, paws in air,
As dreams of snacks make quite a fair.

The trees all chuckle, branches sway,
As squirrels play a prank or two.
They steal the acorns on display,
And giggle low, "What will you do?"

With every rustle, joy prevails,
In leaf-filled jokes and silly tales.
As nature hums her funny song,
The woods echo where we belong.

The Lost Heirloom of the Meadow

In a patch of grass, a map was laid,
For treasures lost and plans displayed.
A fox with glee, a hat so bold,
Said, "I'll find it! Watch me unfold!"

A hedgehog joins with a quizzical glance,
"Is it gold? Oh, let's take a chance!"
They stumble, they tumble, on a quest,
While bickering who's the best.

A turtle trails, moving so slow,
He's got the wisdom, don't you know?
"Just follow me, I've seen the light,
The heirloom's near, just out of sight!"

In the end, they find a prize,
A funny hat, a grand surprise!
They wear it proud, all frolicking glee,
The real treasure? It's friendship, you see!

The Symphony of the Green Heart

In a field where laughter sprout,
The frogs all croak, there's no doubt.
With tiny hats and ties of green,
They form a band, quite the scene.

A caterpillar plays the flute,
While a bumblebee shakes his boot.
The daisies dance, twirl and sway,
It's a wild concert every day!

With each amusing little sound,
The rabbits hop all around.
Their tails a-fluff, they prance in line,
This is the joy of the green vine!

So if you pass by this bright place,
You'll find a smile on every face.
Join in the fun, don't be shy,
Let laughter bloom up to the sky!

Fortunes in the Fronds

They say luck hides in the leaves,
But I found it under my sleeves!
A wise old snail, slow but spry,
Said, 'Check those fronds, give it a try!'

With magnifying glass, I looked around,
Found chocolate coins upon the ground.
But as I reached, a squirrel, quite slick,
Scooped them up with a quick little trick!

I chased that rascal near and far,
To see if I could catch a star.
Instead, I tripped on a grassy mound,
And landed softly, laughter abound!

So here's my fortune, let it be told,
Chocolates are sweet, but laughter's gold.
In every chase or silly tale,
The fun you share will never fail!

The Chronicles of the Blades

In the garden where tall grass bends,
Live the sharpest of all friends.
They whisper tales of wind and sun,
Of battles fought and how they run!

One grass blade claimed he won a race,
Against a snail, who just made pace.
The others giggled, 'Oh what a joke!'
'You're blatantly green, you silly bloke!'

But through the laughter came a shout,
'Let's all go have a dance about!'
So blades together swayed with glee,
Like a wild green symphony!

And in the moonlight, they would prance,
Taking turns in a graceful dance.
The tales they weave are mixed with fun,
In the garden where the races run!

Shadows on the Meadow Path

Under trees where shadows play,
The critters gather, come what may.
A squirrel plays peek-a-boo,
With crafty moves, what can he do?

A rabbit hops with quite a flair,
While turtles trudge without a care.
'Hey, slowpokes!' the sparrows call,
'Join the party, it's a ball!'

They picnic under the boughs so fine,
With crumbs of bread and dandelion wine.
Bugs buzz in with nimble zest,
Creating joy, they're really the best!

So if shadows dance along the way,
Don't miss the fun of this bright day.
For laughter echoes all around,
In those shadows, joy is found!

Beneath the Emerald Canopy

In the shade of green so bright,
Frogs wear hats and dance with delight.
Grasshoppers sing tunes of glee,
As daisies giggle beneath the tree.

Squirrels play tag, all in a rush,
While worms twirl in a muddy hush.
Ladybugs laugh and do a spin,
In this world where silliness begins.

The sun peeks in with a cheeky grin,
As butterflies feast on the fun within.
With snacks of nectar and jokes on repeat,
Nature's party is hard to beat!

Beneath this emerald roof so wide,
Laughter and joy cannot be denied.
So come join the folly, don't be shy,
Under this canopy, watch spirits fly!

Tales from the Clover Patch

Once a rabbit lost his shoe,
And a mouse said, "Now what will you do?"
"I'll hop around on just one foot!"
He laughed, his pride no one could scoot.

A ladybug wore shades so cool,
Claiming, "I'm the best in this school!"
But when the wind came whooshing by,
She tumbled down with a startled cry.

The ants threw a party, loud and clear,
With nuts and crumbs and plenty of cheer.
They danced till the stars began to shine,
In this patch, all fun feels divine.

So listen close to the chatter and play,
In this nook where laughter stays.
For under the sun, each tale unfolds,
In the clover patch, adventure holds.

The Lucky Leaf's Journey

A lucky leaf fell from the tree,
"I'm off to see what I can be!"
It tumbled down with a flirty flip,
Joining the squirrels on a wobbly trip.

"Why don't you bounce?" asked a curious bee,
With honey glimmers and buzzing glee.
"I'd fly, but I can only float,
On breezes soft as a feathered coat."

Through puddles and streams, it drifted along,
Singing a cheerful and whimsical song.
"Let's go meet the flowers in bloom!
I'm off to spread joy, not gloom!"

As sun rays kissed the afternoon bright,
The lucky leaf danced in sheer delight.
With friends all around, it truly knew,
Life's sunny side always shines through!

Resonance in the Wild

In the wild, where giggles arise,
A moose tells jokes under bright blue skies.
The trees stir softly in laughter's wake,
While turtles giggle as they take a break.

Bees buzz in harmony, a musical hum,
As the critters join in, a jubilant drum.
The bushes sway, keeping time with the fun,
A symphony built in the warmth of the sun.

With every rustle, a story gets told,
Of mischief and moments, both silly and bold.
From wriggling worms to the wise old owl,
In this theater of nature, laughter does growl.

So heed the tunes of this vibrant scene,
Where every leaf dances, cheerful and keen.
For in the wild, joy never grows old,
Just listen close, let the fun unfold!

Enchantment of the Green Horizon

In fields where leprechauns dance with glee,
A rabbit sings a tune under a tree.
With socks that clash like colors do,
They sip on rainbows, not one or two.

The daisies giggle and tell a joke,
While mushrooms chuckle, almost woke.
Each blade of grass whispers with cheer,
Creating a symphony for all to hear.

Look out for squirrels wearing hats so fine,
Crafted from leaves, they think they're divine.
They tip their caps to the passing breeze,
Spreading laughter through the forest trees.

With every twist and turn of the path,
Comes a prankster's giggle, a friendly wrath.
So skip along and join the feast,
In this green world, joy is increased.

The Leafy Archive of Legends

In a world where the grass wears a bright green coat,
There lives a wise toad, a self-proclaimed boat.
He sails on puddles, giving advice,
Telling tales of mushrooms that once rolled the dice.

A ladybug plays a tiny lute,
While ants form a band in a leafy suit.
They jam in harmony, a clumsy affair,
While crickets hop by without a care.

A raccoon in glasses reads old scrolls,
Mysteries of acorns, he knows all the goals.
With laughter erupting from each little nook,
Nature's own memoir is one funny book.

So if you wander through bushes and trees,
Don't miss the humor spun in the breeze.
Each leaf holds a tale, a giggle, a grin,
In this leafy archive where stories begin.

The Green Veil of Enchantment

In a forest full of green,
A rabbit danced, so keen.
With a hat that was too big,
He tripped on a leafy twig.

A butterfly, bright and spry,
Said, "Hey, don't be shy!"
He flipped and flapped with glee,
As the rabbit spilled his tea.

The sun peeked through the trees,
Whispering gentle breeze.
"Let's play hide and seek today,"
Laughed the rabbit, hip hooray!

With a roll and a tumble,
He sent the mushrooms a-humble.
"Look, I'm winning!" he declared,
While the forest critters stared.

Tales Intertwined with Ivy

Beneath the ivy's knit embrace,
A hedgehog found a quiet space.
He told jokes to a passing snail,
Who chuckled softly on the trail.

Each tale spun from leafy greens,
Laughter echoed in the scenes.
A squirrel joined, his cheeks quite stuffed,
As the ivy grew a bit too puffed.

A wise old owl blinked twice,
"Let's add some mischief; it would be nice!"
The hedgehog winked, but oh so sly,
While the snail just asked, "Why, oh why?"

As dusk pulled down its curtain bright,
They shared giggles in fading light.
Tales intertwined with gentle cheer,
In the ivy's hold, they drew near.

Lush Secrets of the Meadow

In the meadow, secrets bloom,
A frog croaked by a garden broom.
With a hop, he made a dash,
Leaping over flowers bright and brash.

A bee buzzed in a whirl of fun,
"Come dance with me, it's second to none!"
They twirled beneath a sunbeam's glow,
While a caterpillar moved slow.

The ladybugs began to take flight,
With polka dots shining, oh so bright.
They twirled in circles, round and round,
Creating joy that could be found.

So let's toast to the playful day,
In the meadow, where sweet critters play.
With laughter ringing on the breeze,
Life in the green brings hearts at ease.

In Search of Hidden Luck

Down by the brook, by a rock,
A raccoon searched for the luckiest sock.
With a magnifying glass in tow,
He looked inside each hole and row.

"Is this it?" he grinned with glee,
But found instead a cup of tea.
"A surprise!" he wooped in jest,
For finding luck, this was the test.

Next, he peeked in a toadstool's cap,
Hoping to find a treasure map.
Instead, a mouse began to sing,
To join the search for the hidden thing.

The day wore on with laughter bright,
As they sought luck in pure delight.
In every find, they grinned and played,
For true luck's in the friends they made.

Echoes of the Emerald Realm

In the meadow, frogs wear hats,
Sipping tea, while discussing cats.
The daisies giggle, the thistles dance,
As bumblebees twirl in a clumsy prance.

A snail plays chess with a wise old roach,
Underneath a verdant, leafy broach.
They place their bets on a game of luck,
While a curious worm peeks from the muck.

The rabbits chuckle, wearing shades,
As they gossip about today's escapades.
A squirrel shows off his acorn stash,
But all the while, his secrets flash.

So if you wander through this green land,
Remember to smile and lend a hand.
For laughter erupts in each little nook,
In the realm where the silly never overlook.

A Tapestry of Leafy Legends

On the path, a gnome takes a dip,
In a puddle, he sees his own flip.
With a tiny towel, he wipes his nose,
While all the mushrooms start to doze.

A fox wears boots that are two sizes big,
Dancing silly like a jigging pig.
The daisies join, with their heads all bobbing,
While the grasshoppers find it quite sobbing.

An owl tells tales of a cow in flight,
And how it roamed through the stars at night.
Yet no one knows where that cow may roam,
While crickets sing of a leaf-filled dome.

In this leafy world, joy does abound,
Where the strange and funny are happily found.
So raise a toast to this green brigade,
In the tapestry where laughter's made!

Journeys through the Green Wilderness

A turtle sails in an old tin can,
Trying to catch up with his speedy plan.
But a gust of wind takes him for a spin,
As the daisies chuckle, wearing broad grins.

A bear in a tutu prances around,
While the mushrooms giggle, barely making a sound.
He twirls and he spins, so bright and bold,
Creating a story that needs to be told.

A hedgehog darts with a skateboard flair,
But trips on a twig, sends him through the air.
He lands on a bush, shakes moss from his ear,
And the ladybugs clap, giving a cheer.

So venture deep into this green delight,
Where silliness reigns and smiles are bright.
For in every corner, a quirky tale waits,
In this vibrant realm that joy creates.

Secrets Beneath the Blades

Beneath the blades, a rabbit schemes,
Drawing out plans for his carrot dreams.
With a map made of leaves and a pencil of string,
He devises a tournament for all things spring.

An ant with a mustache gives fashion tips,
As the grasshoppers giggle, doing flips.
They strut their stuff in this leafy parade,
In a world where no frown is ever displayed.

A fox shares gossip among the tall grass,
Of a fish who claims he can fly, what a gas!
They all roar with laughter, their sides feeling pain,
What a wild notion, could it be in vain?

So join the fun in this quirky bazaar,
Where stories are shared under the evening star.
For behind every blade, laughter resides,
In the secrets we keep where whimsy abides.

The Odyssey of Hidden Greens

In a garden where greens conspire,
Lurking 'neath all that wild attire.
A squirrel dons a cap of leaves,
Plotting pranks that none believes.

With every step, a giggle hides,
As rabbits dress in silly strides.
The daisies dance, but don't look down,
They're telling jokes to wear a crown.

Bees are buzzing, what a sound!
Oh, the tales they share around.
A dance-off breaks in sunlight's glow,
With tattered shoes, they steal the show.

So here's to greens with stories bold,
They sidestep woes,they snatch up gold.
In secret quests, they'll find delight,
In every shenanigan, laughter's flight.

Whispers of Green Dreams

In shadows soft where secrets creep,
Whispers float as little ones sleep.
Green dreams twirl like spoons in tea,
With petals playing hide-and-seek.

A grasshopper strums a tiny song,
While fireflies sway, they can't be wrong.
The mushrooms giggle, quite the sight,
As night-time tales take playful flight.

Each leaf a story, bending low,
Hiccups bubbling as breezes blow.
Take heed, dear friend, for laughter's close,
In this realm, it's fun we chose.

So when the stars decide to shimmy,
And plants reveal their tricks so whimsy.
Join the dance, sway with the breeze,
In the twilight, let's be at ease.

Beneath the Four-Leafed Shadow

Beneath the leaves, a secret met,
An eager gnome trying hard to fret.
His tiny hat, a wilted leaf,
His plans for luck met comic grief.

With four-leaf magic on his side,
He trips on roots, slips, and does slide.
The ladybugs laugh, oh what a sight,
As he plots again for his next flight.

Each step he takes, in hopes to boast,
Yet tangled in weeds, he's become toast.
But amid the chaos, he takes delight,
Mistakes turn his woes into pure light.

So if you spot him in the sun,
Join him for tales of silly fun.
Under the shadow of luck's own grace,
Adventure awaits, come find your place.

The Luck of Ferns

In the corners where the ferns grow tall,
A giggling sprite sets to enthrall.
She sprinkles joy, a playful tease,
Baking rainbows, as sweet as cheese.

With every swish, a whimsy shared,
They chant and dance, completely unscared.
A tumble grape, they make it roll,
Giggles erupt as laughter takes hold.

The clumsy snails join in the craze,
Sticky trails form a murky maze.
Still, every bump turns into cheer,
In the green, the spirit's clear.

So if you seek a curious grace,
Find the ferns in their playful place.
And with a smile, let worries wane,
In the luck of greens, joy will remain.

Sprigs of Fortune

In a field where giggles bloom,
Little sprouts burst out with room.
Luck is dancing, jump and sway,
Bringing smiles to every day.

Bumblebees in tiny hats,
Chasing after playful rats.
When luck winks, you can't resist,
Join the fun, you must insist!

With every leaf, a tale is spun,
In this patch, there's endless fun.
Giggling clovers start to tease,
Whispering secrets in the breeze.

So tip your hat and take a stroll,
In this patch, we find our role.
With sprigs of fortune, life's a game,
We laugh our way to famous fame.

Emerald Echoes of Hope

Green whispers tickle at our ears,
Echoes of laughter chase our fears.
Sprightly frogs in bowler hats,
Jumping high like acrobats.

Twirling daisies wear bright grins,
Winning races, everyone wins.
A squirrel high-fives a snail,
In this realm, no one will fail.

Chasing shadows, hopping wide,
In these fields, we take a ride.
Silly dances, a merry show,
Emerald echoes start to flow.

Hope springs forth in every green,
Each giggle makes the world a scene.
Join the fun, don't hesitate,
This laughter's simply first-rate!

Tales from the Clover Patch

Gather 'round for funny tales,
Of four-leafed dreams where laughter sails.
A rabbit juggles carrots fine,
While a turtle sips on wine.

In the clover, secrets hide,
Cheeky whispers, a jaunty ride.
The ladybugs hold silly contests,
For who can wear the silliest vests!

Dancing through days, one must agree,
Laughter is the key, you see.
With each clover, a grin we find,
Wit and whimsy intertwined.

So, pop a joke and spin around,
In this paradise, joy abounds.
Tune your heart to silly pitches,
Let's write tales that know no glitches!

Harvesting Serendipity

In fields where fortune spills with glee,
We gather laughs, just you and me.
With serendipity as our guide,
We take a leap, with hearts open wide.

Jumping jacks in grassy turf,
Unearthing treasures of great worth.
Ticklish breezes brush our toes,
As every turn brings silly shows.

Laughing flowers swirl in zest,
This merry patch is truly blessed.
In every step, surprises bloom,
Even squirrels join in the room!

Harvesting joy, what a delight,
As laughter dances in the light.
Together, we paint a scene so bright,
With every chuckle, we take flight!

Underneath the Clover Canopy

In the shade of leaves so green,
A ladybug plays hide and seek,
While ants march in a straight line,
Discussing snacks, oh so unique.

A snail takes part in a race,
With a worm who is quite spry,
At the finish line, there's cheese,
Or maybe just a pie up high.

The grasshoppers sing their song,
As butterflies dance all around,
A gopher joins the fest so strong,
With jokes that simply astound.

Underneath this playful dome,
Laughter dances on the breeze,
Little friends make it their home,
In a world of giggles and tease.

Legends of Small Wonders

Once a beetle claimed he flew,
But tripped on grass and fell with grace,
Told a tale of his grand view,
Now he's the star of every place.

A tiny frog hops to say,
That shadows dance on sunny days,
He croaks the news in his own way,
And everyone laughs at his plays.

The bees conspire with bright plans,
To win a race though they are small,
With honey sticks and tiny cans,
A sweet surprise that thrills them all.

In every nook, a story's spun,
Of critters who shine like the sun,
Legends shared in the cool dusk light,
As bedtime tales bring pure delight.

The Folklore of the Patch

A squirrel's hat is quite a sight,
Made of leaves and twigs held tight,
He struts around with feline pride,
While mischief squirrels laugh and hide.

The tales of daisies whisper low,
Of dances in the moonlit glow,
With twirls and spins, how flowers sway,
As birds announce the start of play.

A crabapple sits, oh so plump,
Declaring he's the patch's pump,
Tales of juice and laughter flow,
As giggles rise while seeds do grow.

In this enchanted, vibrant space,
Each moment's filled with funny grace,
The folklore of the patch unfolds,
In every heart, a laugh it holds.

Meadows of Serendipity

In meadows where the daisies peek,
A bumblebee begins to speak,
With buzzing tales that always tickle,
Of flower parades and sticky pickles.

A butterfly with colorful dreams,
Plays tag with sunlight's golden beams,
While crickets try to keep the beat,
Each jump a dance, a summer treat.

The grass extends an invite sweet,
For caterpillars to take a seat,
While rabbits giggle, bunnies prance,
They sing their tune, they dance, they dance!

In this whimsical, lively place,
Joy unfolds with every chase,
Meadows bloom with laughter's call,
Where the smallest wonders thrill us all.

The Hidden Folklore of Fields

In fields of green, the tales unfold,
Of luck and laughter, ancient and bold.
A breezy whisper, a jiggle of fate,
Where odd little gnomes hold grand debates.

With every hop, a story's spun,
Of dancing daisies and races run.
The farmer's mischief, the cat's sly grin,
Caught in tales that twist like a spin.

Small treasures bloom in each sprout's gaze,
While bees wear tuxedos for nature's praise.
They buzz a tune, both cheeky and bright,
As rabbits cackle from morning 'til night.

So gather 'round for a giggle or two,
And sing along with the grasshopper crew.
In fields of dreams, we all find cheer,
For hidden folklore is ever so near.

Gardens of Serendipity

In gardens lush, where mishaps bloom,
The vegetables gossip, dispelling the gloom.
Tomatoes hide with a wink and a chuckle,
As cucumbers plot in their leafy huddle.

The sunflowers twist, a jovial dance,
Waving brightly, they take a chance.
With each passing bug, there's a giggle and tease,
Nature's own jesters, aiming to please.

The carrots debate who's the best of the bunch,
While marigolds wear crowns, primed for a brunch.
ComPOSTing stories, they share from the root,
For vegetables know when it's time to be cute.

So stroll through the splendor with a hearty laugh,
In gardens of mischief, enjoy the aftermath.
For serendipity sprouts in every nook,
Where every wise weed is a page from a book.

The Magic of Leafy Fortunes

In leafy realms where luck will play,
Fortunes giggle in a merry ballet.
With each leaf's rustle, secrets arise,
Spilling tales of laughter beneath sunny skies.

The dandelions dance with a wink and a scoff,
Bragging loudly as they scatter and scoff.
While tiny ants march in a silly parade,
In search of a treasure that never has stayed.

A toad croaks jokes that make flowers burst,
While bees do cartwheels through pollen they thirst.
Each petal a jest, each stem has a twist,
In this leafy circus, how could we resist?

So revel in magic, let folly inspire,
For leafy fortunes never tire.
In gardens of giggles, we find our release,
As laughter grows wild, and worries cease.

Secrets in the Shamrock Breeze

In the shamrock breeze, secrets abound,
With whispers of mischief that tickle the ground.
The clouds wear bowties, winks in the air,
As grass blades chuckle, without a care.

Frogs in tuxedos sing silly songs,
While butterflies flit, they can't get it wrongs.
Each gust carries laughter, light as a feather,
In a merry dance, we're all tied together.

The squirrels trade stories of wild acorn heists,
While ladybugs giggle at unforeseen feasts.
With every new leap, a joke's in the breeze,
Entwining our hearts like the roots of the trees.

So let's gather 'round where the wind plays a tune,
And join in the ruckus beneath the bright moon.
For in this breezy treasure hunt, we please,
Find joy in each heartbeat, within the shamrock leaves.

Spirals of Green Enchantment

In a patch of polka dots,
The rabbits played with hats,
Dancing on the lily pads,
While frogs cheered in silly spats.

Bees wore tiny slippers,
Taking giggly hops,
Chasing dandelion wishes,
As the juggle never stops.

Snails held a grand tea party,
With cookies made of clay,
Counting all the raindrops,
That joyfully went astray.

Laughter bounced on breezes,
As the sun wore a grin,
Nature's joyful mischief,
Where every day begins.

Harmony of Nature's Whimsy

The squirrels did a conga,
With a rhythm true and spry,
While the flowers giggled softly,
As butterflies danced by.

A goat tried on some glasses,
And said, "I look so fine!"
He struck a pose for onlookers,
While birds clapped in time.

Clouds were pondering colors,
In a game of hide and seek,
While shadows played tag nearby,
With giggles that couldn't speak.

The sun winked at the daisies,
As they twirled in happy rows,
Creating a bright symphony,
With a song that never slows.

The Shade of Fortune's Kiss

A tree in a jovial mood,
Gave shade to frogs and flies,
Underneath its leafy arms,
There were whispered, silly sighs.

Gnomes on roller skates whizzed,
Down the pathways made of light,
Trading jokes with hidden trolls,
As the stars peeked out at night.

Lemons shared their secret laughs,
While sprouts wore tiny crowns,
Bumblebees debated loudly,
Over silly, sweet-tasting towns.

Rainclouds dressed in polka dots,
Sprinkled dreams with every drip,
While the earth erupted giggles,
In a merry, blissful trip.

Petals of Possibility

In a garden full of whispers,
Petals bounced with glee,
Roses wore red tutus,
As cheerful as could be.

Worms debated worldly things,
From comfy spots of dirt,
While ladybugs played music,
With a beetle for a flirt.

Sunbeams took a lazy stroll,
Painting smiles on every leaf,
While daisies told tall tales,
Of laughter mixed with grief.

As squirrels passed love notes,
Written on blades of grass,
Flowers blushed with happiness,
When the moments came to pass.

Days Beneath the Trifoliate Sun

Three leaves dance in playful glee,
Each twist and turn, oh what a spree!
They laugh and shout with cheeky flair,
In sunny fields, without a care.

A snail joins in, with style so grand,
Wearing shades that make him stand.
The bugs all cheer, the ants applaud,
As laughter echoes, nature's nod.

Beneath the sun, the joy does bloom,
While daisies sway, they find more room.
The triffles whirl, a merry crew,
In split-second games, there's always a new view!

And when night falls, the moon's the jest,
With stars all giggling, they're at their best.
Tomorrow waits with a snicker and grin,
For more tales of fun where the day begins.

Whispers in the Grasslands

The grass is tall, with secrets to share,
Whispers of mischief float in the air.
Bunny ears perk up with surprise,
As chirps and giggles pass by.

A group of bugs holds a meeting discreet,
Discussing their plans for a daring feat.
With crumbs and crumbs, they make a grand feast,
But ends up a riot, oh what a beast!

A crow caws loud, causing dismay,
While ladybugs hide - they're not here to play!
Yet in the grass, shenanigans thrive,
With every tickle, life seems so alive!

Twilight comes, the shadows break,
The fireflies flicker, the soft winds shake.
And as the night brings a chuckling sound,
The whispers continue, round and round!

The Saga of the Lucky Leaf

Once stood a leaf with luck on its side,
Waving at birds that glided and smi
With every breeze, it would flutter and spin,
A jolly old green, with a toothy grin.

It told of treasures buried so deep,
In whispers soft, luring all to peek.
But all they found were worms with a laugh,
That took all the gold for their cozy path!

Through puddles and mud, in mischief they'd play,
With each little jump, they danced all day.
"It's all in the fun!" said the leaf with delight,
As the sun set low, painting the night.

So remember that leaf, oh what a life!
If laughter is gold, you're richer than strife.
For every mishap can bring hearty cheer,
Live each moment, sweeter each year!

Beneath the Canopy of Fortune

Under a shade where the shadows play,
A troop of ants bumbles all day.
With tiny hats and a parade so grand,
They march along, hand in hand.

A squirrel swings in, with acorn in tow,
To join the parade, oh what a show!
"Let's find a feast!" he yells with glee,
While the ants all chant, "Come dance with we!"

A spider weaves jokes with silken thread,
Each punchline leaves them giggling instead.
They tumble and roll, as the sun sinks low,
A carnival grows from the grass below.

As night creeps in, the fireflies twinkle,
A cacophony of laughter that makes hearts tinkle.
For beneath the stars, in this whimsical place,
Fortune favors those with a smiling face!

Green Guardians of the Past

In the garden, tales unfold,
Where green knights brave and bold.
They guard the secrets, oh so sly,
Winking at the passerby.

They wear their armor made of grass,
And dance as squirrels rush past.
With laughter laced in morning dew,
A comedy in green ensues.

Tiny meetings held at dusk,
Conversations full of fluff and musk.
Each rumor spun with leaves in tow,
A symphony of giggles grows.

So here's a toast to verdant cheer,
To Guardians who shed their fear.
In the patch where laughter thrives,
The green delights keep dreams alive.

The Brush of Fortune's Green Hand

Once I found a four-leaf sprout,
Thought it'd change my life, no doubt.
But all it did was wave goodbye,
And left me here to ponder why.

The wind chuckled through the trees,
As if it knew the secrets, please.
A nudge to fate with every breeze,
Encouraging mischief, if you please.

One friendly bug began to grin,
Claimed luck was stored within its skin.
But every time I made a wish,
He'd fly away, oh what a swish!

So here's to fortune's playful art,
That brings together leaf and heart.
In every fold of nature's scene,
Lies laughter, bright and evergreen.

Legends Amongst the Leaves

Beneath the leaves, the whispers stir,
Of legends lost and tales of fur.
A rabbit said with ears so long,
That squirrels sing a tiny song.

Each acorn tells a story grand,
Of daring deeds that took a stand.
The stories tossed on autumn winds,
Where mischief and mirth always blends.

The wise old owl, a skeptic sly,
Mocks tales of how the fireflies fly.
With every glance through twinkling skies,
He winks, suggesting, "Look, surprise!"

So gather 'round this leafy seat,
And cheer for tales both wild and sweet.
In every nook, a laugh appears,
As nature's whimsy sparks our cheers.

Reflections in the Patch

In the patch, where shadows play,
A funny face greets the day.
With petals bright and roots in jest,
Nature's humor is the best.

A wiggly worm joins in the fun,
In the sunlight, they seem to run.
With every giggle, the flowers sway,
Bouncing to the tunes they sway.

The puddles laugh with ripples wide,
Mirroring mischief, none can hide.
So flowers bloom and laughter spreads,
As nature spins its funny threads.

So come and play in green delight,
Where silliness takes off in flight.
Each moment bright, a joy that lasts,
Reflections bright in nature's past.

The Dance of the Leafy Spirits

In a glade where leaves do sway,
A troupe of spirits starts to play.
They twirl in costumes green and bright,
In sunshine's glow, what a sight!

With giggles soft and whispers sweet,
They shuffle nimbly on their feet.
Each toss of hair, a leafy plume,
They jiggle and jive in nature's room!

The acorns laugh, the mushrooms cheer,
As leafy spirits spin with cheer.
A dance so wild, no fear in sight,
Just nature's joy, what pure delight!

Oh, join the fun, don't hesitate,
For leafy spirits celebrate!
With every jig and playful leap,
They spread their magic, oh so deep!

Whims of the Greenwood

In woodlands dense where mischief lies,
The trees exchange their playful sighs.
A squirrel spins a tale so tall,
As giggling flowers watch it all.

The brook chuckles, a cheeky stream,
Reflecting sunlight's sparkling beam.
While bunnies bounce with carefree glee,
In whimsy's grip, they're wild and free!

With shadows dancing, the sun peeks through,
As gossip flows like morning dew.
What capers played beneath the shade,
In laughter's game, no time to fade!

Oh, heed the whispers of the trees,
For whimsy's here upon the breeze.
Every leaf and laugh they share,
Brings joy and fun beyond compare!

The Tale of the Leafy Traveler

A leaf set sail on a breezy day,
Waving goodbye to the roots that stay.
It rode the wind, a tiny boat,
With dreams of places far remote!

Past rose bushes and daisies bright,
In search of fun, oh what a sight!
It wiggled through the fields of gold,
Where tales of laughter all unfold.

Met a beetle with a jaunty hat,
Shared riddles with a charming rat.
Together they danced under the moon,
Making memories, oh how they'd swoon!

At journey's end, back to its tree,
The leaf returned, a heart so free!
With stories spun and laughter shared,
The leafy traveler knew it dared!

A Chorus from the Enchanted Patch

In a garden lush, with colors bright,
The flowers sing in pure delight.
A chorus hums, both sweet and bold,
Of tales and secrets yet untold.

The daisies sway with voices clear,
While roses blush, they hold their cheer.
The tulips tap their lovely feet,
As laughter rises, oh so sweet!

Even weeds join this charming song,
In awkwardness, they still belong.
With every note, a giggle spreads,
In enchanted patches, fun embeds!

So gather round and lend an ear,
For every bloom has stories dear.
In nature's jest and fun-filled patch,
A melody that none can snatch!

In the Shade of Four Petals

Beneath the leaves we sit and grin,
A ladybug does a silly spin,
With four each side, let's take a bet,
Who'll find a lucky leaf first yet?

The acorn jokes, so wise and stout,
Says fortune's hiding all about,
We laugh and chase a wayward breeze,
While dreaming of the tallest trees.

A dandy lion puffs in glee,
To mock the bees: "You can't catch me!"
We cheer 'em on, a buzzing game,
As petals wink and flirt with fame.

So here we sip our herbal brew,
In this green maze, fun bursts anew,
With giggles scattered in the air,
Life's simply grand beyond compare!

Echoes from the Herbal Grove

In herbal nooks where whispers play,
We spill our secrets, come what may,
With thyme to spare and sage on hand,
We plan adventures, wild and grand.

The mint brigade begins a dance,
While basil watches, takes a chance,
To slip a joke beneath the vine,
"Who smells better? You or wine?"

With laughter ringing through the trees,
The rosemary waves, "Oh, do be pleased!"
As willow sways, it cracks a grin,
"The best of fun is found within!"

In this grove where echoes roam,
We carve some fun, we feel at home,
A symphony of chuckles bright,
This herbal haven, pure delight!

Green Tapestry of Fate

In the fields where mischief dwells,
The grass spins tales and giggles swell,
With threads of luck, we weave our day,
As fate's own jester comes to play.

A dandelion, so bold and brash,
Challenges the thistle with a clash,
"Bet you can't make a crow cackle!"
We cheer 'em on in this leafy battle!

A frog in boots croaks out a rhyme,
Proclaims, "I'm winning every time!"
As butterflies gather, all aglow,
In this green weave, we steal the show.

So come, dear friends, and join the jest,
In this tapestry, we love the best,
With nature's threads we laugh and spin,
A happy heart is sure to win!

The Trellis of Tomorrows

On trellis beams, the dreams entwine,
With giggles corkscrewing like wine,
The sunbeams bounce like little sprites,
Inviting all to future sights.

Petunias gossip in a hush,
While lively leaves begin to blush,
"We'll take the stairs to happy days,
And dance forever in sun's rays!"

The wind spins tales of chance and cheer,
Inviting all to hold them near,
With laughter stitched in every seam,
This trellis blooms with every dream.

So lift a cup to days ahead,
And dance until the stars are spread,
In this garden where we all belong,
Let's write our story, laugh our song!

The Hidden Pathways of Luck

In a field where jests roam free,
Tiny wonders hide in glee.
Step lightly on this grassy bed,
Who knows what mischief lies ahead?

A twirl of fate, a dash of chance,
Beneath the sun, the leaves do dance.
A quirky sprite with winks and grins,
Whispers secrets where luck begins.

With every step, a giggle springs,
A bounce of joy, oh how it sings!
Follow the trails of jovial cheer,
You'll find surprises waiting near!

So wander through this maze of mirth,
And stumble onto whimsy's birth.
The hidden pathways lead to cheer,
Where laughter echoes, crystal clear.

Petals and Promises

Scattered petals on the ground,
Whispers of promises abound.
Each one holds a secret smile,
A dash of luck, a dash of style.

With every bloom, a tale unfolds,
Of giggly fables, bright and bold.
Tickling breezes, dancing air,
Let laughter sprinkle everywhere.

A jester's cap, a trail of jokes,
Among the petals, naught but pokes.
Lean in close, and take a peek,
Laughter's winks, they softly speak.

Promises made on leafy trails,
Of silly dreams and playful tales.
So cherish each giggle, every grin,
In this garden where joy begins.

Legends of the Leafy Grove

In a grove where tall tales thrive,
Whimsical whispers come alive.
Frolicking fairies take a bow,
With giggles, tricks, and cheeky wow!

Branches sway with silly flair,
And laughter tumbles through the air.
Every leaf has a story told,
Of jests and pranks, both brave and bold.

A rabbit hops with pompous pride,
In his pocket, a joke to hide.
He jumps and jiggles, pure delight,
Spreading chuckles morning and night.

So step inside, no need to roam,
In this leafy legend, you'll find home.
Where the atmosphere is bright and free,
And every heart sings joyfully.

Emblems of Serendipity

Bright eyes sparkle with sheer surprise,
As quirky moments start to rise.
Emblems of serendipity,
Dance about, wild and free.

A banana peel, a silly slip,
With every fall, a funny flip.
Laughter bubbles like a stream,
In this world of whimsical dreams.

A sandwich sings with voices bright,
Ticklish crumbs in morning light.
Chasing ducks, a merry cheer,
This is where the fun draws near.

So grab a badge of funny fate,
In this land where joys await.
With each new twist, your heart will soar,
In serendipity's playful lore.

Green Pioneers of Hope

In a patch where dreams do grow,
The smallest sprouts put on a show.
With tiny hats and shoes of mirth,
They dance around, proclaiming worth.

They plan a trip to the moon so bright,
With laughter echoing in the night.
"Why not hop instead of walk?"
They cheer, they sing, they play, they squawk!

Their leader, a bold sprig named Keith,
Says, "Life's too short to hide beneath!"
So off they go, with wiggles and twirls,
To paint the sky with leafy swirls.

A parade of green in a world of gray,
They bring the sunshine, come what may.
With giggles that tickle, they jest and cheer,
Here come the pioneers, let's raise a beer!

The Garden of Hidden Gifts

In the garden where laughter blooms,
There hides a treasure of goofy tunes.
With every weed a joke or two,
You'll chuckle till the cows go blue.

The gnomes all giggle as they recline,
Chatting 'bout the best punchline.
With watering cans that spill confetti,
They're planting smiles, all nice and getty.

Sunflowers sway in silly poses,
While daisies giggle in soft doses.
"Why did the carrot blush so red?"
"Because it saw a salad dread!"

From radishes to rows of peas,
The garden's buzzing with such ease.
Let's find the joy that blooms and grows,
Where every patch is where laughter flows!

A Symphony of Leaf and Luck

In the breeze, a whistle plays,
As leaves all join in happy frays.
A symphony of green takes flight,
With giggles woven, pure delight.

The trumpet vines strut their stuff,
While crickets chirp and bluff and puff.
"O say can you see our leafy show?"
A serenade of green, here we go!

They swing and sway on branches high,
Their roots tap dance to the sky.
With every rustle, they strike a chord,
In this grand concert, they're never bored.

A chorus sprouts from every sprout,
Laughter's the tune they can't live without.
Join in their jolly melody,
A symphony of glee, come dance with me!

Beneath the Fronds of Fortune

Beneath the fronds, a tale unfolds,
Of critters bold with hearts of gold.
A beetle sings a merry song,
As ladybugs dance all night long.

With pizza slices made of leaves,
They feast on laughter, joy, and dreams.
"Who stole my crumbs?" a voice does yell,
"It's the squirrel, let's ring the bell!"

They roll in clover, skip and hop,
With giggles that make their worries flop.
"Let's play tag with passing clouds!"
The day is bright, and joy's allowed.

Under the shade, they share their tales,
Of mischief, mishaps, and silly fails.
Beneath the fronds, where fun is ripe,
Fortune smiles with every type!

Green Reveries under the Sky

Under the wide and laughing sky,
Tiny green wonders hop and fly.
They dance with a jig, oh so spry,
While squirrels debate which nut to buy.

Grass blades whisper secrets each day,
Dandelion crowns lead the way.
A ladybug sings, quite in play,
As bees buzz along, never to sway.

The wind tells tales of past delight,
Of mischief at dawn, and bugs that bite.
With every leaf, a giggle takes flight,
In this lively patch, everything feels right.

So join in the fun, let worries slide,
Find joy in the green on this wild ride.
In the laughter of nature, let's abide,
For each leafy moment is magic supplied.

Folklore of the Backyard

In the backyard, tales grow stout,
Of gnomes who wiggle and dance about.
The grasshoppers sing, with no doubt,
While ants march on, like a playful rout.

A cat prances by, wearing a crown,
Claiming the throne, not a frown around.
He chases shadows, flips upside down,
While daisies giggle without a sound.

A puddle reflects the world's bright hues,
Where frogs tell stories and share their views.
Fly away dreams in their tiny shoes,
Under the gaze of the sun's warm cues.

So gather your friends, let laughter soar,
In folklore where life is never a bore.
With magic abounding, who could ask for more?
In this vivid realm, joy is the core.

The Enchanted Field

In an enchanted field so wide and bright,
Where flowers giggle and set things right.
A rabbit consults with a wise firefly,
While mushrooms hold court, oh my, oh my!

Butterflies argue on colors to wear,
While snails boast tales of travels fair.
The breeze whispers fables, light as air,
As crickets compose with flair and care.

With each step taken on this green land,
You'll trip on chuckles, it's truly grand.
Giggling daisies join in a band,
In a world where laughter is quite unplanned.

So come join the fun, don't hesitate,
In this secret field, where we celebrate.
Let joy and whimsy create your fate,
In the heart of glee, we congregate!

Myths of the Meadow

In the meadow's heart, where secrets bloom,
Frogs wear capes, and grasshoppers zoom.
They spin grand myths in the twilight gloom,
Where daisies debate the best flower plume.

A crow acts as judge in a feathered trial,
While rabbits break into a dance with style.
The sun chuckles low, a lazy smile,
As squirrels hold acorn fairs in the aisle.

A wind-blown rumor floats by on a leaf,
Of the dancing flowers, beyond belief.
With petals like bells, they bring great relief,
In the merry meadow, you'll find your chief.

So wander this realm where laughter's the key,
With each little tale shared 'neath the tree.
In myths so sweet, we all can agree,
Joy is abundant, wild, and free!

Echoes of Yesteryear's Green

In fields of green where giggles flow,
A rabbit dance, a funny show.
With glasses perched and hats askew,
The tales he spins, oh where it grew!

Beneath the sun, in grass so bright,
The ladybugs have quite a sight.
They gossip low, on leaves they lie,
About the ants who wear a tie!

A breeze messes with the hair so wild,
Squirrels crack jokes, oh what a child!
With every rustle, a laugh takes flight,
Nature's orchestra, pure delight!

So grab a seat, join the spree,
In shades of green, you're wild and free.
Every nook hides whimsy's cheer,
Echoes of laughter, always here.

Tales from the Secret Garden

In hidden nooks, where shadows play,
The flowers gossip in their way.
A daisy claims she's quite the queen,
While butterflies mark all unseen!

The tulips giggle at the bees,
Who bumble 'round with such unease.
With pollen coats and sticky feet,
They trip on petals, oh so sweet!

A gnome in blue, with painted grin,
Watches the chaos from within.
He whispers tales of pranks and tricks,
As flowers bloom and dance in kicks!

So venture forth, into the spark,
Where petals tell tales, bright and dark.
The garden chuckles, blooms in jest,
With every turn, it's quite the quest!

The Essence of Lucky Foliage

Oh, leaves of green, a vibrant crew,
They trade their tales, both old and new.
A four-leaf found? The crowd goes wild,
While three-leaf clovers mock and smiled.

With every wind, they twirl and tease,
The fungi giggle, swaying with ease.
From roots to tips, the laughter spreads,
As fungi cap their silly heads!

In every patch, a story brews,
Where whispers dance, and chuckles fuse.
The grass joins in, a raucous cheer,
As nature's laughter fills the sphere!

Join the jaunt on a sunny day,
With leaves that dance and laugh, hooray!
In this realm where mirth is bold,
Each green tale, another gold.

Meadows of Hope

In meadows bright, where dreams take flight,
The daisies gleam, oh what a sight!
With giggles springing from each petal,
They plan a race with everyone's mettle.

The clouds above are laughing too,
As butterflies don masks of hue.
They tell wild tales of summer's chase,
While crickets keep the perfect pace!

The wind joins in, with swirls of fun,
Twirling leaves under the sun.
Each blade of grass, a lively cheer,
Whispers of joy, they hold so dear!

So wander forth, in fields of gold,
With every giggle, tales unfold.
In meadows wide, the heart finds glee,
Where hope and laughter roam so free.

A Journey Through the Verdant Veil

In a patch of grass so bright,
A rabbit danced with sheer delight.
He wore a hat that was too wide,
And tripped on roots while full of pride.

With each jump, he'd find a friend,
A turtle slow, on whom to depend.
Together they'd explore the lot,
In a world where laughter couldn't be bought.

A ladybug played tag with glee,
While ants formed a marching spree.
They laughed at clouds that looked like cake,
For fun was all that they could make.

So join the merry, frolicsome crew,
In this green place where joy is true.
No worries here, only silly tales,
On this journey through cheerful trails.

Gentle Stories of Green

Beneath the leaves, a story hides,
Of squirrels that sail on leafy slides.
With acorns as their little boats,
They paddle fast, while no one gloats.

A wise old owl laughs from above,
As hedgehogs dance with heartfelt love.
They spin and twirl, forget the day,
In a world where worries fade away.

A prankster fox steals a shoe,
Leaves it in the pond, who knew?
Frogs wear it as a tiny hat,
Worthy of a stylish chat!

So gather 'round and lend an ear,
For tales of green that bring good cheer.
Where joy is simple, and laughter rings,
In gentle stories that the meadow sings.

The Allure of the Leafy Lane

Down the road where grasses sway,
A pickle jar caught the sun's bright ray.
Inside, a snake with quite the grin,
Wiggled and jiggled to join the din.

A gust of wind brought cheeky sounds,
As bumblebees made silly rounds.
They buzzed and danced, their wings adorned,
In this leafy lane where joy was born.

A hedgehog tips his tiny hat,
To curious pups that bound and chat.
They race for snacks that then go boom,
Exploding with fun, who needs more room?

So take a stroll through this sweet place,
Where every creature wears a face.
In the allure of every green expanse,
You'll find a reason to laugh and dance.

Secrets in the Wind

The wind tells tales, oh so sly,
Of cheeky mice who aim to fly.
With paper wings, they soar and zoom,
In their quest to chase away the gloom.

A dandelion sneezes, puffs away,
Leaving fluffy dreams for kids to play.
They catch the seeds, like stars in flight,
Creating wishes, pure delight.

A grasshopper winks, with silly pride,
As he hears laughter from snails that glide.
They share a joke, a riddle passed,
About the future, and how fast!

Secrets swirl in each soft breeze,
In meadows where the heart finds ease.
So listen close, to nature's song,
In the wind, where all belong.

www.ingramcontent.com/pod-product-compliance
Lightning Source LLC
Chambersburg PA
CBHW051635160426
43209CB00004B/662